fascinations

poems by

Patrick Kindig

Finishing Line Press
Georgetown, Kentucky

fascinations

Copyright © 2025 by Patrick Kindig
ISBN 979-8-88838-889-1 First Edition
All rights reserved under International and Pan-American Copyright Conventions. No part of this book may be reproduced in any manner whatsoever without written permission from the publisher, except in the case of brief quotations embodied in critical articles and reviews.

ACKNOWLEDGMENTS

Grateful acknowledgment is made to the following journals, in which some of these poems first appeared (sometimes in slightly altered form):

The Account	"love & the basilisk" & "adorno/odysseus"
The Collapsar	"cynthia gleason, mesmeric clairvoyant" & "butterfly"
Flyway: Journal of Writing and Environment	"cityscape," "molly," & "in the desert"
Juked	"thumbnail"

I would like to thank Leah Huete de Maines, Mimi David, Christen Kincaid, Kevin Maines, and the rest of the Finishing Line Press team for helping to usher this collection into the world. I would also like to thank the wonderful writers I met during my time in Bloomington, Indiana, where I wrote many of these poems. Particular thanks go to Stacey Lynn Brown, Adrian Matejka, Ross Gay, and Cathy Bowman for their mentorship and support; thanks also to Anni Liu, who provided invaluable feedback on an early version of this manuscript. Thanks most of all to my husband, Derek Granger, for being the most wonderful, supportive spouse I could ever hope for and for developing this book's cover art from a painting by my late grandfather.

Publisher: Leah Huete de Maines
Editor: Christen Kincaid
Cover Art: Derek Granger
Author Photo: Derek Granger
Cover Design: Elizabeth Maines McCleavy

Order online: www.finishinglinepress.com
also available on amazon.com

Author inquiries and mail orders:
Finishing Line Press
PO Box 1626
Georgetown, Kentucky 40324
USA

Contents

candlelight 1

cynthia gleason, mesmeric clairvoyant 2

adorno/odysseus 3

blue 4

revival 8

cityscape 9

mirror 10

t— 11

blanche (wittmann/dubois) 16

dream screen 17

suspension 18

miss g— 19

love & the basilisk 24

butterfly 25

thumbnail 26

blue 27

table(au) vivant 33

lotusfruit 34

in the desert 35

miss g— 36

mannequin 41

apotropaic 42

molly 43

t— 45

for cynthia gleason

candlelight

it blinks to the eye
        a kind of code. the lid

wax, the iris
        an iris: a lesson

for the eye in how
        to be itself. think,

the light says: you
        could be a dandelion

in reverse. think,
        it says: everything

                could be.

cynthia gleason, mesmeric clairvoyant

there is a hand on the loom   &
    the loom is her body

thumb running along
    thumb   a kind of singing

in her veins   at night
    she has learned to sleep

let wool accumulate
    around what she calls

a soul   mornings
    she sees the shore

& the ocean & no
    boats upon it

when   she touches the compass
    on her bedside table

the needle quivers
    & turns   away

adorno/odysseus

a thing for wood
  & leather yes

the body strapped
  & stripped down

what he calls art
  this desire

to be bone
  & negative space

when the need comes
  he is magnesium

touching water
  when it goes

he is magnesium
  one minute later

blue

one summer she lived by the shore with her daughter & her daughter's goldfish & mornings they would dip their toes in the saltwater & laugh & they would go inland & pluck dandelions by the creek watch the white sap rise where the stems broke they would dig into the creek's wet clay & build dams & little temples & they would go back to the house when they got hungry & she would make sandwiches while her daughter played piano what beautiful music people passing on the beach would say they would say how that woman has taught that girl a man owned the house & the shore & the water that touched the shore & when something in the house broke he would fix it thank you she would say as he tightened a bolt thank you for making it out today & he would say no problem honey the wife's in town & i like to keep my hands busy & she would thank him again & her daughter would bring him lemonade in a neon pink cup & he would leave with his hands in his pockets a taste on his tongue a little sour a little sweet sometimes they would come home & he would be there a toothpick between his teeth a leather toolbelt at his hips what she would say as her daughter fed the goldfish what are you doing here & he would stop what he was doing turn around say oh this railing is loose or oh this lightbulb & she would stand there with sap on her hands & dirty fingernails i noticed it last time he would say just want to make sure you're taken care of honey one day he was there & there was nothing to fix what are you doing here is something wrong she asked & he said no he said just wanted some of that lemonade

revival

there is a stage   &
        a woman on it

at her feet   snakes
        & the audience

unlocking its chest
        the woman

contorts her body
        mouth praying

counting stars   she
        breathes   & steps forward

& some part of her
        is in   the air

cityscape

he was looking for his father
        & now   he is not

because of
        the bathhouses

because of   the neon
        & the eyes & the sound

the showers make
        at the y   he looks

at the horizon   sees
        a collection of teeth

if he throws his body forward
        hard enough   he thinks

something will have to
        come loose   have

                to give

mirror

silver & glass
       & inside   an eye

without   a goldfish
     the aquarium is no aquarium

without an eye
     the glass   is just glass

t—

he stands on the boardwalk & looks out & out at the sea no sailors loitering no wolfish men looking for a place to be wolfish just trash & cement & the smell of urine the light's reflection wandering the street behind him & he wondering why he even came in the first place & why he can't seem to go or at least stay gone always coming back to this dirty stretch of shoreline dropping minutes of his life into water by the handful his stomach growing emptier & emptier the sky growing lighter or darker depending on the time of day depending on the weather there used to be cornfields he thinks & the creek flickering through them those long stretches of road that he biked & biked alone & not alone sometimes heading for the abandoned barn or the swamp with its manageable waters & its potential for secrecy sometimes heading home his mother there & his father there or soon to be there until he was not & his mother & the house & the cornfields all receded & the city rose up before him as he rode the greyhound into it as if the bus he was on were a wagon or a chariot as if it were pulled by some animal he knew how to lead he slips out the back door unable to do what that man wanted him to do in the bathroom the stalls with no doors just red velvet curtains & on the street he tells himself he did not come for that he just came to dance black Xes on the backs of his hands a flask of vodka in his pocket he was swigging from it when a queen came in & looked at his hands & said oh honey we've all been there just be careful & kissed his cheek & flipped her braids over her shoulder & disappeared behind the red curtain where the man was waiting the city is full of mouths the man on the street says to him look you've got one i've got one & the earth she's about to swallow us whole you know that don't you the man says then disappears down an alley & he is left alone on the sidewalk running his tongue along the surface of his teeth feeling the cracked molar on the left the filling on the right & when he crosses the street he looks down at the crosswalk & looks up & laughs & says you're right to no one in particular he watches as the man puts a straw between his lips & pulls makes the space of his mouth contract dear god he thinks this shouldn't do what it does to me rattle the windchimes in my chest ring all the bells & as the man takes another sip he has to turn away because he can't bear to look at the man's throat as it moves as his adam's apple raises & lowers itself again & again & instead i will look out the window he thinks i will look at the birds perching on the line & for a while he watches them leave & return & leave & return & it is only after fifteen minutes or so that he realizes he is not looking out the window he is looking at the man's throat & telling himself it is birds & when he raises his eyes to the man's face he sees that he is looking at him & there is a great disturbance in his chest & the blood vessels in his face & all the muscles in his body tighten & untighten & all the pigeons scatter

blanche (wittmann/dubois)

they are looking
        when she undresses

lowers her body
        to the water's

face   the air
        is thick   each mouthful

like blood   like honey   & she
        is like the air   yes

a long wick of radium
        waiting   to be extinguished

as they watch
        her head falls back

spine collapsing
        like a star   & there

in the room   it is white
        it is white   it is white

dream screen

a mountain's green slope
    & before it: a road, banks scattered

with cactus blossoms.
    the blue-haired woman

is on it & she is singing,
    gathering green things

in her arms & singing
    about the shapes earth

can take. valleys, of course,
    & bowls & burial mounds

& hands. sometimes something
    flat & wide. when she opens

her mouth, the mountain
    shivers. the eye watches

until the woman's arms
    are full, until she smiles

& turns toward it, reflects
    its image back to it

with her teeth. then
    her face vanishes & the road

vanishes & the world
    rolls itself up

        like a window shade.

suspension

the eye stares
        at the photos

the one
        recognizable face

weeks pass
        in this looking

& nothing else
        ever

                happens

miss g—

he passes his hand across my eyes & i sleep. outside somewhere i know he is running his fingers down my arms, shaking his hands as if wet. he is smoothing for me the rough edges of my body & i am grateful but not in it. i am off somewhere being a wineglass, a balloon, mostly skin & a lightness inside. when he touches my forehead i know i shiver because he has told me so. when he takes his hand away i am there again, yes, something wrapped around my throat, pulling me to earth.

i saw you last night through your hair. there you were in my fingers & your chest was opening somewhere beyond my eyelids. i could see the wet mess of your heart. it was a muscle, chambered, gunlike. it shuttled your blood & i knew you could not be dead. funny, i thought, how neatly your chest is divided, how each part has its own rhythm. funny, i thought, what an efficient little machine it is.

i saw the girl dying. i saw her in her bed & said she would die & later she did. i said i know death & no one believed me. when i said the girl would die i told them they could stop it, just listen, please, she will die unless you stop it. nobody listened. not one of them did.

they open a pair of scissors between my hands, point a blade at each palm. i can feel the steel feel me, reach its electric tendrils out. there is metal in my blood & it knows it. it wants to touch me, skin to familiar skin. there is movement, then, & a coming closer. & later when i ask if it was me or the scissors, no one will give me an answer.

i understand you. there are distances between us & crossing distances is difficult. there is the sea & what land surrounds it. there is you & me & we are standing on two different planets, such space between. i sleep & cross it, look for your body still well & somewhere. you know i could find it if you'd let me. you know i could.

love & the basilisk

the eye opens toward it, feels
        its glossy edge

nudged. then: something
        deeper, an electric ray

in its veins, denaturing
        blood. the eye

wet clay, the eye
        permafrost: earth

& ice & a waiting
        for spring. it knows

this waiting
        is a parlor trick: now

you see it, now
        you see it. look

away for one second & now
        you see it & see it

              & see it.

butterfly

near the piano she lifts   a knee
       unruffles   her ruffles

& pinned to her dress
       a bright two-hearted flame

when she is dead
       she knows

she will not be able   to do this
       so she opens the window

leans against
       the frame

when her body catches   the breeze
       it is almost   as if

             it were breathing

thumbnail

opal opening downward
        & then an edge: sudden

moment of air. on
        the cutting board: less

& less. a mouth
        entering the pink, becoming

part of it. see
        the keratin teeth unzip

themselves, a kind
        of smile. see the hand

become a face, one
        red tongue

                spilling out.

blue

& later that day he was still there after the lemonade after a whiskey & soda after she said well it was nice seeing you but i'd better get dinner started & he sat at the kitchen table as a storm blew in from the water well he said as the rain came down & the ocean came up & the driveway erased itself in the dark i'd better not drive in this no he said an empty glass in his hand i'd better take the couch okay

& then in the dark he was there honey he said honey & the clock on the mantle was making noises & through the window the ocean was making noises too & she woke up & said no said what is happening honey he said honey & the needle in her chest spun round & round & she said wait wait she said this is when her hair changed when she became the woman with hair like that afterward they stayed at the shore a while longer but the man did not come anymore he sent a note that said sorry that said the wife but she did not read it only saw these words as they disappeared as the blue flame of the gas stove swallowed them this is when she began her wandering when she picked up her habit of looking at people too hard & too long & making them feel something about it & of course she did this alone she could not do it when her daughter was there so she left her daughter and her daughter left her a distance growing between them that they took like medicine in small doses & then large ones filling their bodies' cavities with what they needed to & her daughter never understood why never understood how she had lost her mother or how her mother had lost herself why she avoided water & mirrors & polished bronze why she could not look at herself why nobody else could look at her but that night by the shore her daughter was there she was watching through the glass egg of the fishbowl & the goldfish was in the bowl a low gold star swaying before her swimming & swimming & behind it she saw her mother on the bed moving then unmoving the goldfish there between the girl & the woman & afterward the girl forgot it all until years later a man with a gold pocket watch said look at it look at it swim back & forth & breathe in & breathe out & relax & the girl looked at it & she saw it swimming there between herself & the man & she closed her eyes & said oh

table(au) vivant

she is there & so is
        the vanity. the

brush, the pigment, the thumb
        running along

each lid: what creates
        the eye's careful

smoke. her collected gestures
        like a clock, one turn

& then another, one pupil
        dilating in the skull's

warm dark. her knees
        brush the oak above

& it hums, hurls
        its many parts against

hers. something here
        is fluttering, flapping

its wings. something here
        is alive & on fire.

lotusfruit

   & now   an amber glass
        the eye's   bright needle

   when it tells him   to drink
        he drinks   &

   the waterfront
        crawls   away

in the desert

there is a reason the aliens
   chose here the world

at its largest in the sun
   & in the rain the eye

looking   back
   to the plateau's face to

the place the earth's rim
   once was & here

there is a way the body
   dissolves becomes

a dream of contact
   of touching lightly

the inner thigh &
   the eye

sheds it all peels
   the eggskin around it

the redrock
   growing now enormous

becoming for miles
   the only real thing

miss g—

once they did it without my knowledge. i sat by the fire & two of them looked at me & i was gone, their eyes dipping into me like water. they touched & troubled me, fingered the surfaces of my skull. when i returned they would not tell me who had been inside. i smiled & smiled, said yes, what a funny joke that was. & later i walked the streets & threw rocks through all their windows, broke all the glass in town.

your absence feels like copper, like bronze, & at night i sit in the dark & hammer it. the work is fine & it takes a long time. when i finish i will have a necklace or a bracelet or an ornate goldfish. but i am sure you know that i will never finish it.

i am the best they have ever seen. they pinch & poke me, stick needles in my thumbs. & still i will not move, will not scream. what a marvel, they say, lifting a bright candle to my eye. what a marvelous woman this woman is.

i will not sit where they tell me to sit. i will not give my hand to this man. i will not go into the other room & undress, get into bed. i will not wait six minutes to wake. i will not drink water & call it rum. i will not drink rum & call it ammonia. i will not raise my arm when they point at it & squint. when they point at my chest i will not stop breathing, no, i will not.

remember: you would touch me & i would shiver & i knew it. your bones were lodestones, irresistible. in the house i knew where you were. in bed i tasted copper. when you cut your hair it lingered in the kitchen, clung to my bare feet. there were things your body did to my body that neither of us could explain. when i touched you you were hard & cold & it is true that i could never stop touching you. yesterday i grabbed a doorknob & i could have sworn it was your hand.

mannequin

in the shop window
        he sees   a head

blue wig askew   chin
        inclined

& below   bare plastic
        the face too

soft brown shine
        a vague   curving

the sunlight touches
        her chest   there are

two cavities   where
        her lungs should be

apotropaic

the amber beads
      at her throat: there is

a smell to them, earth
      & heat at the back

of the mouth.
      she wears them

at night, near
      open flames. when

men ask
      to cup them, she

pulls away. when
      the blue-haired woman

asks, she lets her
      cradle them, roll

the beads across
      her thumbpads. lets

her see each one
      etched with a small god,

see herself turn
      & walk away

molly

yes   he says
     & yes   & yes

his eyes   expanding
     & devouring   yes

the men   yes
     the dancing   the bodies

dancing   yes
     yes   the skin glossing

yes   frosting
     with salt   yes

&   in the bathroom
     yes   in the aluminum

stalls   each aperture
     glorious   yes

gloriously opening
     yes   yes   like a tulip

yes   into lips
     & bodyheat   yes   yes

there a part of him   yes
     goes   must go   yes

yes   yes   &
     he sees   yes

his face   in the metal
     yes   in the burnished

wall   yes
     until   he exhales

yes   yes
        & then   he does not

see it   yes   yes
        & then   yes

it is gone
        yes   yes

t—

the man hands him a wineglass & in the light he can see something inside small shapes growing smaller swimming through the wine like dandelion spores like goldfish drink up the man says & lowers himself to the couch knee to quivering knee & so he does he drinks & knows as he is drinking what this means what will happen shortly to his body how the wine & what is in the wine will enter his blood & do what it is meant to do & the man is there watching & smiling as he swallows as he pours the whole glass down his throat & says yum there used to be cicadas he thinks & a ringing in the trees that made them electric the wind was there too but you couldn't hear it over the buzz & hum that sound that burrowed its way into your skull & stayed there laid its eggs how easy it is to bend your knees he thinks to bend your body to another man's will to do what another man wants & want it too at the coffeeshop he sits & stares at the club he dances at the streetcorner he waits for the light to change even when no one else is waiting at the liquor store he buys liquor at home his mother sits & waits & is probably working on another quilt at the laundromat he thinks of her as he separates his lights & darks at the city's various cathedrals he thinks of her & averts his eyes at the boardwalk he likes to think his father is thinking of him though he knows this is not the case at the foot of his bed he does pushups & situps & flexes his wet muscles before the mirror at night he sleeps & dreams of horses of the boy who used to live next door who let him ride his horse sometimes who once looked at his hands & his feet as he guided the animal forward then looked him in the eye & said you're a natural he remembers his first birthday in the city how he bought himself vodka & a birthday cake & he drank the vodka & put candles on the birthday cake & blew them out he said to himself you must not cling to your boyhood any longer he looked in the mirror in the dark & said it's time you were a man & he ate one slice of cake & threw the rest out & he drank the whole fifth of vodka because he could now really who was there to tell him he couldn't not his mother not his father not even the law & this made him feel giddy & sick as if he were standing at the edge of a very high cliff deciding whether to take a step forward or take a step back & he looked in the mirror & saw his eyelids sagging beneath the weight of the alcohol & said do it he said looking into his own eyes do it do it

References

Henry Adams, *The Education of Henry Adams*. 1907. Houghton Mifflin Company, 1961.

Theodor W. Adorno and Max Horkheimer, *The Dialectic of Enlightenment*. Translated by Edmund Jephcott, edited by Gunzelin Schmid Noerr, Stanford University Press, 2002.

Sybille Baumbach, "The Medusa's Gaze and the Aesthetics of Fascination." *Anglia*, vol. 128, no. 2, 2010, pp. 225-45.

Maurice Blanchot, *The Space of Literature*. Translated by Ann Smock, University of Nebraska Press, 1982.

Stephen Connor, "Fascination, Skin and the Screen." *Critical Quarterly*, vol. 40, no. 1, 2003.

Andreas Degen, *Ästhetisches Faszination: Die Geschichte einer Denkfigur vor ihrm Begriff*. Walter de Gruyter GmbH, 2017.

Joseph Phillipe Francois Deleuze, *Practical Instruction in Animal Magnetism*. Translated by Thomas C. Hartshorn, B. Cranston & Co., 1837.

Robert C. Fuller, *Mesmerism and the American Cure of Souls*. University of Pennsylvania Press, 1982.

Alan Gauld, *A History of Hypnotism*. Cambridge University Press, 1992.

Homer, *The Odyssey*. Translated by Robert Fagles, Penguin Classics, 1996.

James Joyce, *Ulysses*. 1922. Dover Publications, 2009.

John B. Newman, *Fascination, or the Philosophy of Charming*. Fowler and Wells, 1881.

Emily Ogden, *Credulity: A Cultural History of US Mesmerism*. University of Chicago Press, 2018.

Charles Poyen, *Progress of Animal Magnetism in New England. Being a Collection of Experiments, Reports, and Certificates, from the Most Respectable Sources. Preceded by a Dissertation on the Proofs of Animal Magnetism*. Weeks, Jordan and Co., 1837.

Harriet Prescott Spofford, "The Amber Gods." *"The Amber Gods" and Other Stories*, edited by Alfred Bendixen, Rutgers University Press, 1989.

John Rechy, *City of Night*. 1963. 50th Anniversary Edition, Grove Press, 2013.

Gertrude Stein, "Melanctha." 1909. *Three Lives*. Project Gutenberg, 2005.

Ann Taves, *Fits, Trances, and Visions: Experiencing Religion and Explaining Experience from Wesley to James.* Princeton University Press, 1999.
Tennessee Williams, *A Streetcar Named Desire.* Signet, 1947.
Tom Van Imschoot, "Surviving Fascination." *Image & Narrative,* vol. 14, no. 3, 2013, pp. 151- 68.
Brigitte Weingart, "Contact at a Distance: The Topology of Fascination." *Rethinking Emotion: Interiority and Exteriority in Premodern, Modern, and Contemporary Thought,* edited by Rüdiger Campe and Julia Weber, de Gruyter, 2014, pp. 72-100.

Patrick Kindig is the author of the chapbook *all the catholic gods* (Seven Kitchens Press 2019) and the micro-chapbook *Dry Spell* (Porkbelly Press 2016) as well as the academic monograph *Fascination: Trance, Enchantment, and American Modernity* (Louisiana State University Press 2022). His poems have appeared in the *American Poetry Review*, the *Cincinnati Review*, *Colorado Review*, *Washington Square Review*, *Copper Nickel*, and other journals. He currently lives and teaches in rural Texas.

www.ingramcontent.com/pod-product-compliance
Lightning Source LLC
Chambersburg PA
CBHW030059170426
43197CB00010B/1593